1535

Anne Boleyn is beheaded. Henry marries Jane Seymour.

154?

Henry marries Catherine Parr. Mary I and Elizabeth I made heirs after Edward to the throne.

1540

Henry marries and divorces Anne of Cleves, then marries Catherine Howard.

1533

Henry marries Anne Boleyn in secret and Elizabeth I is born.

1542

Catherine Howard is beheaded.

1537

Edward VI, Henry's only son, is born and Jane Seymour dies.

1547

Henry VIII dies and Edward VI is crowned king.

Map of royal birthplaces

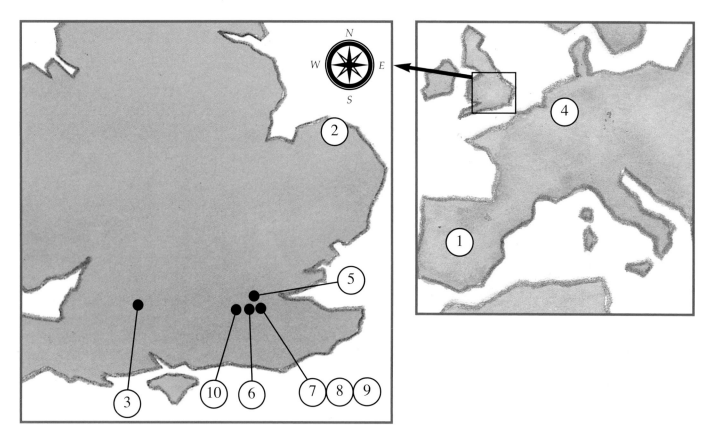

1. **Catherine of Aragon** (16 December 1485): Archbishop's Palace, near Madrid, Spain
2. **Anne Boleyn** (c. 1501): Blickling Hall, Norfolk
3. **Jane Seymour** (c. 1509): Wolf Hall, Savernake Forest, Wiltshire
4. **Anne of Cleves** (22 September 1515): Düsseldorf, Germany
5. **Catherine Howard** (1520): Lambeth, London
6. **Catherine Parr** (1512): Blackfriars, London
7. **Henry VIII** (28 June 1491): Greenwich Palace, Greenwich (now in London)
8. **Mary I** (18 February 1516): Greenwich Palace, Greenwich
9. **Elizabeth I** (7 September 1533): Greenwich Palace, Greenwich
10. **Edward VI** (12 October 1537): Hampton Court Palace, Middlesex

Timeline of Henry VIII's life

1491

Henry VIII is born.

1516

Henry VIII's first daughter, Mary I, is born.

1526

Henry VIII becomes interested in Anne Boleyn.

1531-1535

Henry becomes head of the Protestant Church of England.

1509

King Henry VII dies. Henry VIII becomes king and marries Catherine of Aragon.

1520

Henry VIII and Francis I of France plan a great tournament at the Field of the Cloth of Gold, to show off their wealth and majesty.

1527-1531

Henry asks Pope for divorce from Catherine of Aragon and banishes her from court.

Author:

Fiona Macdonald studied History at Cambridge University and at the University of East Anglia. She has taught in schools, adult education and university, and is the author of numerous books for children on historical topics.

Artist:

David Antram was born in Brighton in 1958. He studied at Eastbourne College of Art and then worked in advertising for 15 years before becoming a full-time artist. He has illustrated many children's non-fiction books.

Series creator:

David Salariya was born in Dundee, Scotland. He has illustrated a wide range of books and has created and designed many new series for publishers both in the U.K. and overseas. In 1989 he established The Salariya Book Company. He lives in Brighton with his wife, the illustrator Shirley Willis, and their son Jonathan.

Editor:
Karen Barker Smith

Assistant Editor
Stephanie Cole

Published in Great Britain in MMXIV by
Book House, an imprint of
The Salariya Book Company Ltd
25 Marlborough Place, Brighton BN1 1UB
www.salariya.com
www.book-house.co.uk

PB ISBN-13: 978-1-909645-27-1

SALARIYA

© The Salariya Book Company Ltd MMXIV

1 3 5 7 9 8 6 4 2

A CIP catalogue record for this book is available from the British Library.

Printed and bound in Singapore.

Visit
www.salariya.com
for our online catalogue and **free** interactive web books.

PAPER FROM
SUSTAINABLE
FORESTS

You Wouldn't Want to Be Married to Henry VIII!™

Written by
Fiona Macdonald

Bah! Women!

Illustrated by
David Antram

A husband you'd rather not have

Created and designed by
David Salariya

BOOK HOUSE

a SALARIYA imprint

Contents

Introduction   5

Risky royals   6

Your only career – marriage!   8

Wife no. 1: The brother's bride   10

Rejection!   12

Wife no. 2: Bewitching!   14

Failure!   16

Off to the Tower!   18

Wife no. 3: Third time lucky?   20

Wife no. 4: Fat Flanders mare!   22

Wife no. 5: Young and foolish   24

Wife no. 6: Happy at last   26

What happens next...   28

Glossary   30

Index   32

Introduction

The year is 1542, and times are difficult in England. King Henry VIII, who has ruled England since 1509, is getting old, tired and dangerously unpredictable. He has quarrelled with the Pope, leader of the Catholic Church in Rome, encouraged raids on Church property and arranged the murders of people who have displeased him. His private life has been scandalous – he has had five wives so far, and all of them are now dead! Now he is thinking of getting married again.

Your name is Catherine Parr and you are an attractive, intelligent and devout widow. Your father was a senior royal official at the court, so you know members of the royal family and you understand their ways. However, you are still shocked and frightened by the news that King Henry VIII wants to marry you! What should you do? Would you want to be married to King Henry VIII?

Risky royals

Will you or won't you?

HENRY VIII, KING OF ENGLAND is tall, strong, energetic and fond of hunting, music and dancing. He used to be handsome but is fast becoming fat and diseased. He is very passionate and can be ruthless.

You must soon give Henry VIII an answer to his proposal of marriage. This is no easy choice. Many people would say, 'Be warned!', and would advise you to steer clear of the English royal family and of all the clever politicians at the royal court. Many hopeful, ambitious men and women have enjoyed a brilliant career there – but many of these careers have ended with prison, or, worse still, death! There are many people you should be very wary of.

Watch out for:

intrigues · plots · secrets

ARCHBISHOP CRANMER. Protestant scholar and religious leader.

EDWARD SEYMOUR. Soldier, politician and keen Protestant.

JOHN DUDLEY. Top courtier and Protestant supporter.

DUKE OF NORFOLK. Leader of an ancient noble family. Catholic supporter.

6

Handy hint

Think carefully! If you offend the king by refusing to marry him, he could make your life very miserable.

Hmmm...

Of course she'll say yes - I'm irresistible!

MINISTERS OF STATE.
The royal government is run by ministers who are clever, ambitious and unscrupulous. Don't upset them!

Your only career – marriage!

The alternatives:

BECOMING A NUN is no longer an option. Two years ago, Henry VIII closed down the nunneries as part of his plan to reform the Catholic Church and seize its wealth.

DON'T BE FOOLED by flattery from the men at the royal court. They all flirt with pretty women and are not to be trusted. You don't want to get a bad reputation!

Blush! Simper!

Yo have already been married twice before – sadly, both your husbands died. Compared to many Tudor women, however, you have been lucky. Your family didn't force you to marry a man you hated or arrange your marriage just to make money. Nevertheless, as a Tudor teenager, you soon abandoned all hopes of having a handsome boyfriend and settled for men approved by your family, who were respectable, wealthy – and dull.

However, now that you are a middle-aged widow, you can decide for yourself who to marry next time. Will you choose King Henry VIII? Before making your final decision, read on to consider the fate of his five previous wives.

BE ESPECIALLY CAREFUL to avoid marrying a poet or a musician, however talented. They often come from humble backgrounds with no money and no political allies.

Wife no. 1: The brother's bride

King Henry VIII's first wife was a Spanish princess called Catherine of Aragon. In 1501, she was sent to England to marry Henry's older brother, Prince Arthur. However, Arthur died less than a year after his marriage, leaving Catherine a widow at the age of 17. The English royal family did not want to upset Catherine's father by sending her home, so they arranged for her to marry Henry instead! The wedding took place in 1509. In the same year, Henry became King. Henry and Catherine were both good-looking and clever. Catherine was also gentle and sweet-natured – everyone liked her.

Henry

ARTHUR looked like a promising match for any princess, until, as a teenager, he fell seriously ill.

HENRY grew up to be stronger, fitter, and much more glamorous than Arthur, his older brother.

CATHERINE, however, had no say in the matter of her marriage. She just did as she was told.

King

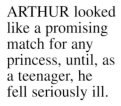

THE ROYAL FAMILY had to ask the Pope for permission for Henry to marry his dead brother's widow, as this was against church law.

Messengers

Pope

PRINCE HENRY was only 11 when Arthur died. He had to wait several years until he could marry Catherine. He grew up knowing that one day she would be his bride.

Rejection!

For almost 20 years, Henry and Catherine were happy together. However, they had one problem – they had no sons. Although they had six children, only one, a girl called Mary, survived. Henry grew increasingly desperate for a male heir, who could be King when he had died. In 1526, he met a young lady-in-waiting called Anne Boleyn and fell madly in love with her. He decided to leave his wife to marry Anne, hoping that she would give birth to a boy. Henry asked the Pope to annul his marriage to Catherine. He argued that he should no have married his brother's widow after all, and that his lack of an heir was a punishment from God.

ANNE BOLEYN was mysterious, elegant and charming. People called her 'fascinating', suggesting that she used magic powers to attract the King.

CATHERINE protested that there were no valid reasons for ending their marriage. Henry was very angry and banished her from the court. She never saw him or their daughter, Mary, again.

Catherine's father *Pope* *Henry*

PRINCESS MARY was shocked at her mother's treatment. She was also angry with her father and fearful for her own future. Her only consolation was her strong Catholic religious beliefs.

THE POPE was now caught between powerful rivals – King Henry VIII and Queen Catherine's family in Spain.

Wife no. 2: Bewitching!

After five long years the Pope still refused to annul Henry's marriage to Catherine. In the end, Henry decided that he could wait no longer. In 1532, Anne finally agreed to be Henry's lover and quickly became pregnant. In 1533, Henry declared that his marriage to Catherine had never legally existed, whatever the Pope might say, and that Anne was now his real, lawful wife. All Europe was shocked when, in the summer of 1533, a very pregnant Anne Boleyn was crowned England's new Queen.

AT FIRST Anne resisted Henry's advances. She would not have just a casual love affair. She wanted to be Henry's wife – and the Queen of England.

EVENTUALLY Anne got her way – Henry married her secretly in 1533, once she was pregnant. Henry hoped that her baby would be a son and heir.

Bring back Queen Catherine!

It's a disgrace!

Down with Anne Boleyn!

Handy hint

NEW LAW

If you do become Queen, you can persuade the King to make new laws. But don't expect them to make you popular!

ENCOURAGED BY HENRY and his new Queen, Protestant reformers preached against the Pope and all Roman Catholics, including Catherine of Aragon's family in Spain.

Failure!

Once Anne Boleyn had married Henry VIII, she had two vital duties to perform: to keep him happy and to produce a male heir. In September 1533, her first baby was born. It was a girl, Elizabeth. Henry was bitterly disappointed and blamed Anne. Anne tried to convince him that their next child would be a boy, but Henry was already getting fed up with her. Anne became pregnant again in 1534 and in 1535, but both babies died. King Henry still did not have a son. Once again, he began to fear that his misfortune was a punishment from God – he decided that Anne's babies died because she was a witch and because she had been unfaithful to him.

Humph! What use is another girl?

ANNE'S BABIES probably died because she had a blood condition that killed them in the womb.

Handy hint

Don't talk to ANY man – even your brother. The king will suspect you of being unfaithful!

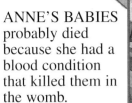

Knackered!

It's shocking!

They say she's a witch!

ANNE BOLEYN had many enemies, including members of rival noble families, Henry VIII's political opponents, supporters of Queen Catherine and people who did not want religious reform. They all accused Anne of terrible crimes, including witchcraft and adultery.

17

Off to the Tower!

In 1536, Queen Catherine died. This meant that Henry VIII was free to marry again according to the Catholic Church, which had refused to recognise his marriage to Anne all along. Henry thought that if he married a third time, this time with the Church's blessing, maybe God would at last send him the son he so badly wanted. He had Anne sent to the Tower of London and put on trial for adultery. While Anne was in the Tower of London, Henry was already flirting with his next girlfriend. She was a young noblewoman called Jane Seymour.

Predictably, Anne was found guilty of everything Henry accused her of – no-one wanted to defy the King! She was beheaded on 19 May 1536. She had failed in a royal wife's most important duty – she had not produced a male heir. She paid the price for this failure with her life.

Anne's fate:

OFF TO THE TOWER! Anne was locked up in the Tower of London and kept under armed guard.

ON TRIAL! She was accused of treason and adultery, found guilty and condemned to death.

TORTURE! Her brother and her male friends were cruelly tortured and then killed.

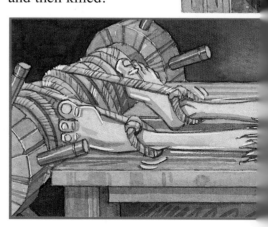

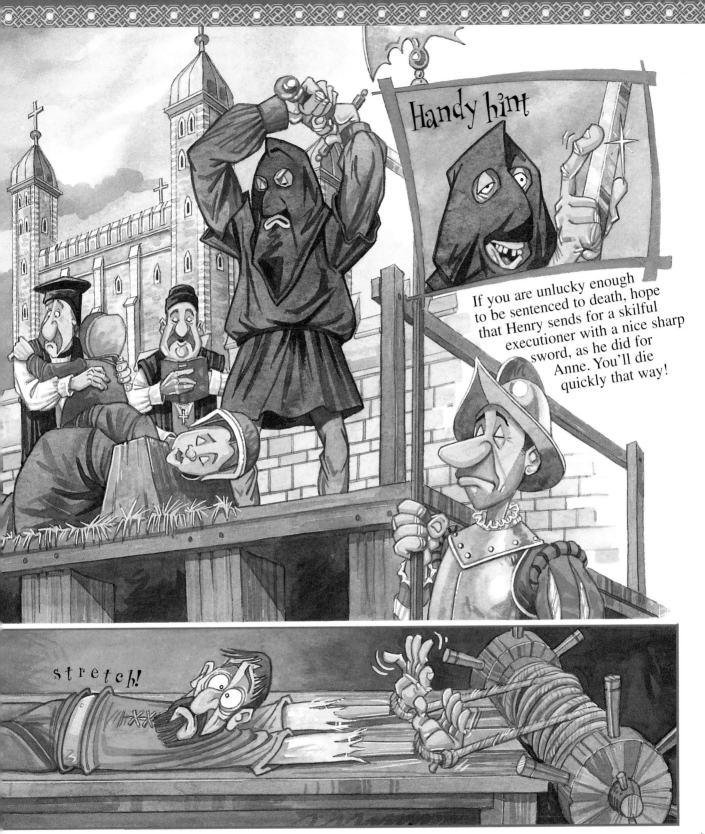

Handy hint

If you are unlucky enough to be sentenced to death, hope that Henry sends for a skilful executioner with a nice sharp sword, as he did for Anne. You'll die quickly that way!

stretch!

Wife no. 3: Third time lucky?

HENRY LOVED JANE, but his proposal to her was also prompted by his strong desire for a baby son. He was fed up with daughters!

Two days after Anne Boleyn was executed, Henry VIII married Jane Seymour. Like Anne Boleyn, she refused Henry's advances until he promised to marry her. Also like Anne Boleyn, she was encouraged by her family to attract the king. They hoped to win power and influence.

JANE tried unsuccessfully to reconcile Henry with his daughter, Mary.

Jane

Mary

HENRY hoped that Jane would give birth to plenty of children, at least one of whom would be a son and the heir to the throne!

You're going to grow up to be just like your Daddy!

Jane Seymour had been a lady-in-waiting to both Catherine of Aragon and Anne Boleyn, so she knew what Henry was like. He was now getting old (almost 40). He was also very fat, unhealthy and hot tempered. He was a dangerous man to disagree with! However, Jane wanted to be queen. Her married life was not easy, but worse was to come. Jane soon became pregnant and in 1537 she gave birth to a healthy baby boy, named Edward. Here, at last, was Henry's longed-for son! However, sadly, Jane died just a few days afterwards.

Handy hint

Don't be born into a politically-ambitious family. They'll use you to try and win power for themselves.

Yes, poor little thing!

Wife no. 4: Fat Flanders mare!

King Henry had an heir at last. However, he still needed a wife, to provide more sons and to carry out official duties at court. His advisors suggested Anne, daughter of the Duke of Cleves. As Henry had never met Anne of Cleves, he sent the artist Holbein to paint her portrait. He liked the result and asked Anne to marry him. However, when Henry met Anne, he was horrified by her appearance and even called her a 'fat mare from Flanders'! To avoid offending her father he went ahead with the wedding, but he arranged a separation straight afterwards. Anne accepted Henry's offer of a pension and went to live peacefully in a comfortable house in a quiet country town.

CLEVES was a state close to France and Flanders. Henry hoped that Anne's father would be his ally against France and Spain.

What an ugly woman!

Flanders

22

AFTER THE WEDDING Henry and Anne kept as far apart from each other as possible. They both looked forward to the time when their 'marriage' could be annulled.

Handy hint

If your new husband doesn't like you, keep calm! Don't make a fuss! Then you can end your marriage in a peaceful and friendly way.

What an ugly man!

Flutter

Swish!

Pant

Wife no. 5: Young and foolish

CATHERINE HOWARD had a reputation as a flirt long before she married King Henry VIII.

A fter his experience with Anne of Cleves, Henry wanted to find beauty and excitement in his next wife. He found both in the teenager Catherine Howard, a lively and pretty lady-in-waiting at the royal court.

Catholics

Protestants

CATHOLICS were pleased with Henry's marriage to Catherine. They hoped it would stop the king's planned church reforms. Protestants were less happy.

ARCHBISHOP CRANMER had the unpleasant task of telling Henry about Catherine Howard's love-affairs.

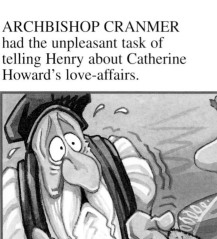

Catherine was charming but she was also foolish. She didn't love Henry, who was twice her age, but she wanted to be queen. She spiced up her loveless royal marriage by having secret love-affairs with handsome young men. News of these romances soon spread throughout the royal court. Henry was furious and ordered swift and terrible punishment for Catherine. After just two years of marriage she was beheaded, at the age of 21.

LIKE OTHER QUEENS, Catherine was beheaded. In some ways, she was lucky. According to the law, she could have been burnt alive.

Well - here goes another one...

Wife no. 6: Happy at last

It's beef broth, today!

After carefully considering the fates of Henry VIII's first five wives, you decide to marry Henry VIII after all! Your wedding takes place in 1543 and your marriage lasts for four years, until Henry's death in 1547. It is a great success, in spite of Henry's serious illness (he is plagued by ulcers on his legs), his unpredictable temper and the 21-year age gap between you. You nurse Henry devotedly during his last illness and you also look after Henry's three children by his previous wives. Henry allows you to continue your studies and your interest in new Protestant religious ideas, even though he does not agree with all your views.

SCHOLARLY WIFE. You are intelligent and well educated, speaking Latin, Greek, French and Italian. Even though Henry is your third husband, you have always found time to study.

KIND STEPMOTHER. You have no children of your own, but you take great care of Henry VIII's children – Mary, Elizabeth and Edward. You hire top tutors to teach them history, languages, music and religion.

There, there.

Handy hint
The King's a man like any other. He needs tenderness and loving care.

AFTER HENRY VIII'S DEATH, you marry Lord Thomas Seymour, who has been in love with you since before you met the king.

YOU DIE aged 37, after the birth of your first child. You are deeply mourned by all who knew you.

Divorced

CATHERINE OF ARAGON
1485-1536
Married to Henry VIII
1509-1533

Beheaded

ANNE BOLEYN
c.1501-1536
Married to Henry VIII
1533-1536

Died

JANE SEYMOUR
c.1509-1537
Married to Henry VIII
1536-1537

All three of Henry's children become kings or queens. Edward is the first to rule, because he is the only son. His reign is brief and because he is so young, advisors rule for him. They introduce many Protestant Church reforms. After Edward's death, Mary becomes queen. She's a Catholic and has many Protestants burned at the stake – her harsh religious policies make her unpopular. Elizabeth is Henry's last child to rule and she is the most successful. Remembered today as one of England's most glorious queens, her long reign (almost 50 years) proves that a woman can rule as well as a man despite what Henry VIII thought!

Divorced   Beheaded   Survived

ANNE OF CLEVES
1515-1559
Married to Henry VIII
6 months in 1540

CATHERINE HOWARD
1520-1542
Married to Henry VIII
1540-1542

CATHERINE PARR
1512-1548
Married to Henry VIII
1543-1547

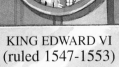

QUEEN MARY I
(ruled 1553-1558)

Married King
Philip of Spain
but had no children

KING EDWARD VI
(ruled 1547-1553)

No marriages
or children

QUEEN ELIZABETH I
(ruled 1558-1603)

No marriages
or children

THE END OF THE TUDORS

Glossary

Adultery Being unfaithful to a husband or wife.

Annul To cancel.

Archbishop Religious leader; head of the church in a particular country.

Banished Sent away from (usually as a punishment for wrongdoing).

Catholic (or Roman Catholic) church One of the main branches of the Christian church. Its headquarters are in Rome and its head is the Pope. Until the 16th century, almost all Christians in western Europe were Roman Catholics.

Courtier A man or woman who works at or spends time at a royal court.

Flanders The old name for land that today forms part of Belgium and the Netherlands, both in north-west Europe.

Heir Someone who will inherit (take over the ownership of) property or a title after the death of a relative.

Lady-in-waiting A woman (usually from a noble family) who acts as a trusted personal servant to a member of the royal family.

Nun Member of a religious community of women that live according to strict religious vows.

Pension Money paid to someone who has retired from work.

Pope Religious leader and head of the Roman Catholic Church.

Protestant Member of a Christian group that broke away from the Roman Catholic Church in Tudor times. Protestants disagreed with Roman Catholics over the way worship was organised and the way the Church was run.

Radical Deep and thorough.

Reformers People who try to bring about changes in a society.

Tower of London A large castle in London – during the time of Henry VIII, prisoners seen as enemies of the King were held there.

Treason Betraying your country to an enemy. In the past in England, the word was also used to describe the behaviour of a wife who was unfaithful to her husband.

Tudor A dynasty (ruling family) whose members were kings and queens of England from AD 1485-1603. Also used to describe the period of history when Tudor kings and queens ruled.

31

Index

A
adultery 17, 18, 30
Aragon, Catherine of 10, 12, 14, 15, 17, 18, 21, 28
Archbishop Cranmer 6, 24
Arthur, Prince 10

B
beheadings 18-19, 25
Boleyn, Anne 12, 14, 15, 16, 17, 18, 20, 21, 28

C
Catholic Church 5, 8, 18, 31
Catholics, catholicism 12, 15, 24, 28, 30
Church law 10
Cleves, Anne of 22, 23, 24, 29
court 5, 6, 8, 12, 22, 24, 25
courtiers 6, 30

D
dancing 6
Dudley, John 6

E
Edward 26, 28, 29
Elizabeth 16, 26, 28, 29
Europe 14, 30

F
Flanders 22, 30
France 22

G
God 12, 16, 18
government 7
government ministers 7

H
heirs 12, 14, 16, 18, 22, 30
Holbein 22

Howard, Catherine 24, 25, 29
hunting 6

L
ladies-in-waiting 21, 24, 30

M
Mary 12, 20, 26, 28, 29
music 6
musicians 8

N
Norfolk, Duke of 6
nunneries 8
nuns 8

P
Parr, Catherine 5, 26, 29
Philip, King of Spain 29
poets 8
politicians 6
Pope 5, 10, 12, 14, 15, 30
prison 6
protestants, protestantism 6, 15, 24, 26, 28, 31

R
reformers 15, 31
Rome 5
royal family 5, 6, 10

S
Seymour, Edward 6
Seymour, Jane 18, 20, 21, 28
Seymour, Thomas 27
soldiers 6
Spain 12, 15, 22

T
torture 18
Tower of London 18, 31
treason 18, 31

W
widows 5, 8, 10, 12
witchcraft/magic 12, 16, 17

Top people at Henry VIII's court

Thomas Wolsey (c.1472–1530) was the son of a butcher from Ipswich in Suffolk. By 1515 Wolsey was both a cardinal and Lord Chancellor of England. Almost as rich as the king, he employed 1,000 people and lived in great luxury at Hampton Court Palace near London. Wolsey's failure to get the king a divorce led to his sacking in 1529. He would probably have been executed if he hadn't died en route from York to London in 1530.

Thomas More (1478–1535) trained as a lawyer and was a wily statesman and a celebrated scholar. His book describing an imaginary ideal society, *Utopia*, was a best-seller. More was knighted in 1521, and followed Wolsey as Lord Chancellor in 1529. More fell out of favour with the king after he refused to acknowledge Henry as supreme head of the Church of England, and he was executed in 1535.

Thomas Cromwell (1485–1540) was clever and rose up through the ranks to become Henry's chief minister in 1534. A ruthless politician who made many enemies, Cromwell was behind the king's decision to make himself head of the English Church. In 1540, Cromwell pushed Henry VIII into marrying Anne of Cleves. When the marriage ended in disaster, his political opponents encouraged the king to have him arrested. Cromwell was beheaded in 1540, though in later life the king bitterly regretted ordering his death.

Richard Rich (1496–1567) was a thoroughly nasty piece of work. He became Henry's top legal advisor and carried out his dirty work, such as extracting confessions from the king's political enemies. He played an important part in the downfall of both More and Cromwell. A man of few principles, Rich skilfully moved with the times. He became a baron under Edward VI and later helped Mary I round up heretics.

Henry VIII's diseases

King Henry was horrified by disease and he spent every summer moving around the south of England to avoid the dreaded sweating sickness (known in Europe as 'the king of England's disease'). But this didn't stop him coming down with one health problem after another:

- **Age 22:** Henry catches smallpox but is not scarred by it.

- **Age 33:** Henry suffers his first attack of malaria, which plagues him for the rest of his life.

- **Mid-30s:** Henry nearly drowns after falling headfirst into a muddy ditch while out hunting. He is saved by a quick-thinking footman.

- **Age 35:** A jousting accident leads to ulcers on both legs. In the king's later years, the pain becomes so severe that he often cries out in agony. The treatment is just as horrific: the ulcers are regularly cut into and dressed with an ointment that contains lead. This poisons Henry's blood and, probably, gradually affects his mind.

- **Age 39:** Henry hurts his left foot playing tennis.

- **Age 44:** Another jousting accident knocks the king out for two hours. By now his fits of rage are made worse by lack of sleep, sore throats and terrible headaches.

- **Age 45:** Henry develops a painful growth on the side of his nose. Due to his diet, Henry is now also suffering from severe diabetes and dropsy, which causes his whole body to swell up.

- **Age 50**: Henry catches tertian fever. Symptoms include hot and cold flushes and sweaty fits, leading to violent behaviour every other day.

- **Age 55:** Henry spends the last eight days of his life in bed, surrounded by the awful pong of his bursting leg ulcers.

- **After death:** Henry's bloated corpse is said to have exploded two weeks after his death. When the lead casing of his coffin burst, stray dogs wandered into St George's Chapel, Windsor, and licked up the blood that spilled out.

Henry's children

Edward VI

Unfortunately, Henry's only son and heir was a sickly child – and he was crowned at just nine years old. He was deeply religious and was determined to turn England into a thoroughly Protestant land. Before he could secure his plan, Edward died, aged 15, of an unidentified lung disease.

Mary I

Next in line was Henry VIII's elder daughter, Mary. She saw herself as the true heir to the throne, as she believed that her mother's divorce from Henry VIII was illegal. She was fervently Roman Catholic, and determined to save her Church from Protestantism.

In 1554, she married Philip II of Spain and tried to help in his wars against the French, but she only succeeded in losing Calais in 1558 – England's last foothold in France. When she died, childless, at the age of 42, many in England rejoiced.

Elizabeth I

The youngest of Henry VIII's children came to the throne in 1558: Elizabeth, the 25-year-old daughter of Anne Boleyn, and a Protestant. She was charismatic and wise, but could also be ruthless. Elizabeth I's reign of 45 years is seen as a 'golden age' in which Britain prospered, and grew in self-confidence as a world power.

Mary I and Philip II of Spain

Did you know?

The English were known as gluttons in the rest of Europe, and Henry VIII set the example – one feast at Greenwich Palace lasted over seven hours! The 200-strong kitchen staff at Hampton Court provided meals of up to 14 courses for some 600 people in the Great Hall. Many dishes were designed to show off the king's wealth and power.